A-Z Of Random I
Sports Editio

By Jack Lexington

**Copyrighted September 2017
By Jack Lexington**

Table of Contents

Introduction..4
A Is For....American Football...5
B Is For .....Basketball..14
C Is For....Cricket..24
D Is For....Darts..27
E Is For.....Eton Fives...33
F Is For....Football (Soccer)...34
G Is For.....Golf..40
H Is For....Horse Racing..45
I Is For.....Ice Hockey..49
J Is For...Jokgu..54
K Is For....Kubb..55
L Is For.....Lacrosse..57
M Is For....Motocross/Supercross..59
N Is For....Netball...64
O Is For....Orienteering..68
P Is For...Polo..70
Q Is For....Quoits..74
R Is For....Rugby (All Disciplines)...75
S Is For....Snooker..82
T Is For....Tennis..86
U Is For....Ulama..90
V Is For.....Volleyball...92
W Is For.....Weight lifting...95
X Is For....Xare..97
Y Is For....Yukigassen..98
Z Is For...Zui Quan..99

Introduction

I have decided to do a series of fact books as a follow-up to the original 'A-Z Of Random Facts'. Each book in the series will follow the same format as that book However, each will focus on a particular topic. Such as sports, politics, places, arts and culture, history and more.

This Book will focus on sports from around the world and will include facts such as world records in that particular sport.

So I hope you enjoy this mini-series and learn one or two little things you may not have known

A Is For....American Football

1; A man from North Carolina owns the only video recording of Suoer Bowl I. He is unable to sell it after the NFL withdrew an offer of $30,000 and refused to buy the tape they also cautioned the man he will face legal action if he sells it to another buyer.

2; Guns and feminine hygiene products are banned from their adverts by the NFL.

3; In 2014 a $400m 5 year deal was struck between the NFL and Microsoft, the deal made the Microsoft Surface the official NFL tablet.

4; The NFL threatened to take legal action against any churches that threw Super Bowl parties

5; In 2015 Sarah Thomas became the first female official in the NFL.

6; NFL rules state a football field must be built facing North or South, or in the shade.

7; After upsetting Denver Bronco fans Brian Bosworth managed to sell 10,000 t-shirts to them at $15 each with the slogan "Ban the Boz" without them knowing that "the Boz" himself as selling them.

8; The NFL sued insurance lawyers to recover the money lost when they had claims brought against them for failing to protect players against brain injuries.

9; The 1982 NFL season was cut to a 9 games per team league thanks to the 57-day player strike.

10: The Minnesota Vikings mascot, Ragnar. Is the only human mascot in the NFL

11; During the 1987 season, another player strike was held. During this period teams used replacement players.

12; Over the last 50 years there are 4 teams that have never been to the Super Bowl. They are the Cleveland Browns, Detroit Lions, Jacksonville Jaguars and the Houston Texans.

13; The Waterboys from the NFL make an average $53,000 annual salary.

14: The NFL cannot host games on a Friday or Saturday as College football takes place on these days. Federal Laws prohibit the two competing on the same day.

15; Bill Belichick is the only NFL coach who refuses to be involved in any John Madden video game.

16: In 2010 Brett Favre became the only player still active in the NFL to have a grandchild.

17; Not all the proceeds of the "Breast Cancer Awareness Month" goes to charity only around 5-10% of the money actually does.

18; Kenny Washington was the first African-American in the NFL.

19; Terry Crews used to paint his teammates' portraits.

20; In 1971 Chuck Hughes became the only player to have died on the field.

21: The 1972 Miami Dolphins are the only team to win the Super Bowl with a perfect record.

22; Out of a 3-hour TV coverage, the average NFL game only has just over 10 minutes of action. Around 1 hour is spent on adverts the rest is spent on the likes of huddling and replays.

23; NFL Cheerleaders are paid $50 a game.

24; Tom Dempsey who was a kicker for the Saints owns the record for the furthest NFL field goal (63 yards) what makes this more impressive is that he was born with a club foot.

25: Marcus Allen is the only person to ever win a Heisman Trophy, College Football National Title, NFL MVP, a Super Bowl & Super Bowl MVP.

26: ESPN pays the NFL $102m per game for the rights to show it on their channel.

27; Packers Rookie Randall Cobb is the first person to play in the NFL who was born in the 1990s

28; Like the WWE the NFL is legally recognised as an entertainment brand rather than a sport.

29; The NFL made video game company EA remove features from its game such as end goal celebrations and realistic crowds.

30; For the past 10 years, there have been no white cornerbacks on any NFL roster.

31; if an NFL game is tied the result is decided with the flip of a coin,

32; The NFL does not pay taxes as it is considered a Not-for-profit organisation.

33; The Green Bay Packers are the only non-profit NFL team, and they are owned by its group of 112,000 fans.

34; During the 1958 NFL Championship Game, an NBC Employee posing as a fan ran onto the field to delay the game because the national television feed went dead.

35; it takes 3,000 cows to provide enough leather for a years supply of footballs to the NFL.

36: Steve Smith leaves his cleats on the field after every game. This is to raise awareness about homeless people without shoes.

37; If some NFL teams don't sell enough tickets for a home game, they won't broadcast the game within a certain radius of the stadium, thereby forcing people nearby to buy tickets to see the game.

38; Players have been fined up to $5,000 in the past for giving a game ball to fans.

39; The first team in the NFL to have cheerleaders was the Pittsburgh Steelers.

40; 68% of stadium works that have occurred in the NFL have come from taxpayers money.

41; The Super Bowl is the most watched TV event in the USA.

42; The team with the shortest lifespan in the NFL(1 game in 1921) is the Tonawanda Kardex Lumbermen

43; The NFL owns the licensing rights to every team except the Cowboys. In 1995 Cowboy's owner Jerry Jones started to make his own deals, NFL sued him for 300 million, to make the league back down, Jerry counter-sued them for 750 million.

44; American Football derived from English sports Rugby and Football(soccer).

45; In 1983 Dallas Cowboys running back Tony Dorsett became the only player to ever rush for a 99-yard touchdown

46: The G on the helmet of the Green Bay Packers stands for Greatness.

47; Baltimore Ravens got their name from Edgar Allan Poes' "The Raven" Baltimore is the place where the poem was written. The team mascots are named Edgar, Allan and Poe.

48; The last scoreless game occurred in 1943 between Detroit Lions and New York Giants

49; The first recognised game took place in 1869 using rules similar to rugby. It was between Princeton and Rutgers Universities.

50: The huddle was invented by Paul Hubbard who was legally deaf and huddled the players close, so he could hear them better

51: Soldier Field in Chicago is the oldest NFL stadium that is still in use

52: Around 80% of Super Bowl tickets go to corporate sponsors.

53: The shortest NFL player was Jack "Soapy" Shapiro, who was 5'1" and weighed only 119 pounds. He was a blocking back for the Staten Island Stapeltons in 1929.

54: Helmets only became a legal requirement in 1939.

55: Super Bowl XXX Was the first to be broadcast in Navajo (A Native American language)

56: To be eligible for the Hall of Fame a player must be retired for at least five years.

57: Joe Montana was the NFL's 82nd draft pick in 1979.

58: In 1977 quarterback Bob Griese became the first player to wear glasses during a game.

B Is For …..Basketball

1: A teacher named James Naismith invented Basketball in 1891

2: The first Basketball hoops were just peach baskets.

3: The Boston Celts have won the most championships with a total of 17

4: Michael Jordon holds the playoff scoring record with 5,987

5: In 1982 the first basketball game was played with only 1 point scored in the whole match.

6: The height of a basket is 10ft

7: Basketball became an Olympic event in Berlin 1936.

8: International basketball is played at 10mins per quarter whereas the NBA is played with 12mins per quarter.

9: The NBA was formed in 1949 after two leagues merged together. The National Basketball League(NBL) and the Basketball Association of America (ABA).

10: Kareem Abdul-Jabbar holds the record for most career points scored. After a 20-year career, he scored 38,387 points.

11: In the early 1900s basketball games were played in cages of chicken wires and mesh.

12: Originally basketball teams had 9 players.

13: During a 1977 court fight between the Los Angeles Lakers and the Houston Rockets, forward Kermit Washington nearly fatally punched forward Rudy Tomjanovich. "The Punch," as it has been called, dislocated Tomjanovich's jaw and caused spinal fluid to leak from his brain. He recalled tasting the fluid in his mouth.

14: The backboard was invented after fans kept interfering with shots. The baskets used to be nailed to the mezzanine balcony of the courts.

15: Up until the 1950s footballs(soccer balls) were used to play basketball.

16: According to ESPN the best female basketball player of all time is Diana Taurasi

17: In 1967 dunking was banned as backboards were being shattered.

18: Giannis Antetokounmpo is the tallest point guard in NBA history with a height of 6' 11".

19: The first women's basketball uniforms were called Bloomer Suits.

20: The Philadelphia 76ers are so named because the declaration of independence was signed there in 1776.

21: The tallest basketball player in the world is Paul Sturgess who stands at 7'8"

22: Dribbling did not become a major part of basketball until the 1950s.

23: A warm basketball has more bounce than a cold one.

24: The Cleveland Cavaliers hold the record for most consecutive league losses (26) which they set in 2010-11.

25: The Cleveland Cavaliers also hold a more positive record. That is the biggest margin of victory which they set in 1991 beating Miami Heat by a score of 148-80.

26: Michael Jordan's Air Jordan's are the best-selling basketball shoes of all time.

27: Since 1974 the official NBA basketballs have been made by Spalding

28: On a Spalding basketball there are 122 bumps per inch.

29: Rasheed Abdul Wallace holds the record for technical fouls with 317.

30: The smallest ever basketball player was Tyrone "Muggsy" Bogues who was 5'3".

31: The Sacramento Kings retired the number 6 in honour of their fans known as "The sixth man"

32: The oldest franchise in the NBA by just under 20 years are the Sacramento Kings who were formed in 1923.

33: The highest ever attendance at a basketball game is 108,713.

34: All basketball uniforms are manufactured by Adidas.

35: The shot clock was invented by a man named Danny Blasone.

36: The LA Lakers hold the record for the longest winning streak with 33 games in 1971-72.

37: Robert Parish has played the most games in history. He played 1,611 games in a 21-year career.

38: The best 3 point shooter in the history of the NBA is Ray Allen who made 2,973 3-point shots

39: You must be 19 in the same calendar year as the draft to play in the NBA.

40: The player who is silhouetted in the NBA logo is former LA Lakers star Jerry West.

41: Salt Lake City is the smallest city with an NBA franchise.

42: Wilt Chamberlain holds the record for the most points scored in one game he scored 100 points for the Philadelphia Warriors in their 169-147 win over the New York Knicks in March 1962.

43: All NBA courts are made of maple wood.

44: The first ever NBA game as won by the New York Knicks. The defeated the Toronto Huskies 68-66

45: In 2016 Stephen Curry led the Golden State Warriors to a record-breaking 73 wins.

46: In 2016 Stephen Curry became the only player in NBA history to be voted the seasons MVP By a unanimous vote.

47: In 1949 Joe Fulks known as 'Jumping Joe Fulks' Introduced the jump shot.

48: In October 1979 Chris Ford became the first ever player to score a three-point basket in the NBA.

49: In 2014 Brittney Griner became the first woman to dunk in a WNBA playoff.

50: Pete Maravich is the all-time leading scorer in men's college basketball he scored 3,667 points in only 83 games.

51: At the age of 23 LeBron James became the youngest player to reach 10,000 points in the NBA.

52: Meadowlark Lemon was known as 'The Clown Prince' Of the Harlem Globetrotters.

53: As a child NBA coach Frank Vogel appeared on 'Late Night With David Letterman' in a segment about human tricks. Frank Vogel's trick was brushing his teeth while spinning a basketball on the toothbrush.

54: During his 14yr career Wilt Chamberlain never fouled out.

55: Kevin Durant chose the number 35 because his first coach Charles Craig was murdered at the age of 35.

56: Michael Jordan won the Nestle Crunch Slam Dunk contest in February 1988 with a perfect score of 50.

57: Jerry West sank a 60ft shot on the buzzer in April 1970. To help tie the game between the LA Lakers and the NY Knicks. Unfortunately for him, his team lost in overtime.

58: In April 2001 Wang Zhizhi became the first Chinese player to appear in the NBA.

59: In 2016 Stephen Curry's mouth guard (Found by a fan) was sold at auction for $3,190.

60: Kareem Abdul-Jabar has on the most league MVP's in history with 6.

61: Stephen Curry and Klay Thompson were nicknamed "The Splash Brothers".

62: In his debut NBA game LeBron James scored 25 points.

63: German-born Dirk Nowitzki is the highest scoring foreign-born player in the NBA.

64: Due to his speed and athleticism Clyde Drexler was known as "Clyde the Glyde"

65: The first college basketball game had 9 players on each side.

66: Larry Brown is the only coach to win both an NBA title and a NCAA national championship.

67: When Michael Jordan came out of retirement he wore the number 45. This was for three reasons. 1) His number (23) had been retired. 2) He ore 45 while playing minor league baseball. 3) His brother wore 45 in High School.

68: The Detroit Pistons originally came from Fort Wayne, Indiana.

69: Stacey Augmon was known as the plastic man.

70: The first professional basketball league (NBL) was won by the Trenton Nationals.

71: Former commissioner Larry O'Brien had the NBA trophy named after him.

72: Julius Erving is the only player to be voted MVP in both the ABA and the NBA.

73: The Houston Rockets were founded in San Diego.

74: Dick Motta was the first head coach of the Dallas Mavericks.

75: John Stockton holds the record for most career assists in the NBA with 15,806.

76:: in October 1973 Elmore Smith set the record for most blocked shots in a single game with 17.

77: In 2001 Lisa Leslie became the first player in the WNBA to win all 3 MVP awards in a single season.

78: The NBA record for most career disqualifications is held by Vern Mikkelsen.

C Is For....Cricket

1: Chris Gayle was the first person to hit a six from the first ball in a test cricket match. He achieved this feat in 2012.

2: Cricket originated in England when first playing around wool was used as a ball.

3: The first recorded cricket game took place in 1646

4: In the early days of the sport people were fined for missing church to play cricket.

5: In the 1760s it as considered normal to pitch a ball this is why the shape of the bat changed from curved to straight.

6: The longest match in history took 14 days to complete. It was in 1939 between England and South Africa and the match ended in a tied game.

7: Rain and bad light are the most common causes for interruptions to a cricket match.

8: There are 3 umpires in each cricket game. Two on-field and 1 off-field.

9: There was a cricket match that got interrupted because a pig ran onto the field.

10: The wicket gets its name from the small gates found on cricket playing grounds.

11: Cricket was the first ever game to be played in the USA using a bat and a ball.

12: A cricket bat weighs around 2-3 pounds.

13: A cricket ball is made of cork wrapped in a string with an outer layer of leather.

14: Cricket balls used in the men's game weigh around 5.5 ounces. This is slightly heavier than those used by younger players and women.

15: Rounders was inspired by cricket. This, in turn, evolved into baseball.

16: A score of 111 is called a Nelson. This is considered to be an unlucky score.

17: The first test match took place in 1877.

18: The first men's twenty20 match was played in 2005 between Australia and New Zealand.

19: There are 10 reasons you can be dismissed in cricket.

20: The first ever day-night test match was played in Adelaide from 27th November to 1st December 2015, between Australia and New Zealand, using a pink ball.

21: A British team is the only nation to win an Olympic cricket contest (in 1900), becoming the only Olympic gold medallists in cricket, and therefore the current Olympic Champions.

D Is For....Darts

1: Darts can trace its origins back to battlefields in the late 18th Century. It as a fun pastime for soldiers to throw small arrows at the trunk of a tree.

2: England holds the record for most consecutive world championships with 7 between 1977-1991.

3: John Lowe was the first man to win the World Championship in 3 separate decades.

4: John Lowe was also the first man to achieve a 9-dart finish in a televised match. This occurred in 1984

5: There is no age barrier with darts.

6: Before dart boards were made of cork they had been made of both elm and clay.

7: The maximum length a dart can be is 12 inches.

8: The reason darts use a flight is to prevent the rear of the dart overtaking the front of the dart.

9: Darts was first shown on British TV in 1962.

10: The first 9-dart finish in the PDC as struck by Dutchman Raymond van Barneveld. He achieved this in 2009.

11: In a game of 501 there are 3,944 ways to achieve a 9-dart finish.

12: Phil Taylor holds the record for most titles he has 16 across both disciplines (BDO, PDC) he has 14 in the PDC and two in the BDO

13: Phil Taylor has reached more finals than any other man with an impressive 18.

14: Once again that man Phil Taylor holds the record for most match wins with 105.

15: Phil Taylor also has the longest winning streak with 44 matches.

16: The highest number of maximum scores(180) in any one tournament is 704 this happened in 2017.

17: Gary Anderson holds the record for the number of 180's in a single tournament he achieved 71 in a tournament in 2017.

18: Gary Anderson also holds the record for the most maximum scores in a single match with 22. This again as achieved in 2017.

19: Phil Taylor has made the most PDC championship tournament appearances with 24.

20: Phil Taylor was born in Stoke-On-Trent, England

21: 23 is the lowest number that cannot be scored with a single dart.

22: James Wade won the 2007 World Matchplay tournament It was his first televised tournament trophy.

23: Phil Taylor was born in 1960.

24: The Bullshooter World Championship electronic darts was held annually in Chicago.

25: If you get a single double and treble of one number that is called a Shanghai.

26: Phil Taylor is known as "The Power".

27: The centre of the dartboard is at a height of 68 inches from the floor.

28: The World Series of Darts tournament was replaced by the US Open in 2007.

29: A competition dartboard is made of compressed bristle.

30: The 2003 Windy City open as held in Lincolnwood Illinois.

31: The throwing line is known as the Oche.

32: The term Oche comes from the Old French meaning "Cut a deep notch in".

33: In a game of cricket if a player hits 3 trebles it is known as a "White Horse".

34: In 1990 Phil Taylor won his first World Championship by defeating Eric Bristow.

35: A hat-trick is 3 bulls-eyes.

36: Both players throw a dart aiming to get nearest the bull in order to see who throws first. This is called the diddle.

37: The World Darts Council (WDC) was formed in 1992.

38: Las Vegas was the first city in the USA to host the World Cup of Darts.

39: Phil Taylor won the world championship 7 years in a row from 1995-2003.

40: The highest score you can win a match with using 3 darts is 170 (Treble 20, treble 20, bulls-eye)

41: The score of 26 (20, 5, 1) is known as Bed and breakfast.

42: In 2001 Phil Taylor had his nomination for an MBE taken away after he was convicted of indecent assault.

E Is For.....Eton Fives

1: Eton Fives is a handball game similar to Rugby Fives.

2: Eton Fives is played on a 3-sided court.

3: The object of the game is to stop your opponents hitting the ball in an upwards direction off the wall before it bounces twice. (Similar to squash rules).

4: Eton Fives originated in the 1800s in the UK at Eton College. The chapel at the college is what lends it's shape to the court.

5: Tom Dunbar hold the record for most Kinnairds' on with an impressive 13 two ahead of his nearest rival John Reynolds.

6: The captain in Eton Fives is known as the keeper.

F Is For....Football (Soccer)

1: Football is the most popular sport in the world.

2: Football originated in China around 476 BC.

3: The largest Football tournament consisted of no less than 5,098 teams. They competed in 1999 for the second Bangkok League Seven-a-Side Competition. Over 35,000 players participated.

4: Manchester United's former manager Alex Ferguson was fired from a previous job at Scottish club St. Mirren in 1978 for swearing at a lady.

5: A match in Argentina played between 5th tier sides Claypole and Victoriano Arenas ended with the referee Damian Rubino, brandishing 36 red cards he sent off all the players on the field and a mix of subs and coaches.

6: The first televised football match was an Arsenal practice match it took place in 1937.

7: Pakistan manufactures around 80% of the footballs in the world.

8: The professional football used today has been the same for over 120 years it is 28 inches in circumference.

9: The most goals scored by a single player in a single match is 16. This was achieved by two players. In December 1942 by Stephan Stanis while playing for Racing Club de Lens against Aubry Asturies in the French Cup. And in May 2007 Panagiotis Pontikos achieved the same feat in the third division of the Cypriot(Cyprus league) while playing for Olympus Xylofagu against Ayios Athanasios.

10: Nawaf Al Abed scored the fastest goal. It occurred in the Sudi Arabian league and was scored in 2 seconds.

11: Goalkeepers did not have to wear different coloured shirts to outfield players until 1913.

12: Footballers run on average 10kms per game

13: The very first football club was founded in 1857 by Nathaniel Creswick and Major William Priest it was called the English Sheffield Club.

14: Neil Armstrong wanted to take a football to the moon. This was disallowed by NASA as they deemed it to be un-American.

15: There are 27 teams in the world who take their nick-names from Beatles songs.

16: in 1998 Lightning killed an entire football team in Congo.

17: A European country has reached the final of every World Cup except for 1930 and 1950.

18: At junior level Brazilian legend Ronaldinho scored 23 goals in one game.

19: The first black professional football player was Arthur Wharton who played from 1885-1902.

20: The Brazilian legend of the game Pele was the first to describe football as "The Beautiful Game".

21: In Peru, in 1964 a riot was caused that killed over 300 people. What as the catalyst? A referees decision during a football game.

22: Ivory Coast team ASEC Abidjan went unbeaten for 108 games between the years of 1989 and 1994.

23: Former player and current manager Mark Hughes once played for Bayern Munich and Wales on the same day.

24: Alvin Martin scored a hat-trick he achieved this by scoring past three different goalkeepers in the same match. He achieved this for West Ham against Newcastle in 1986.

25: Italian defender Giuseppe Bergomi never played in a world cup qualifier but appeared in 4 World Cups.

26: Despite playing for 6 clubs who have on the Champions League Zlatan Ibrahimovich has never actually on it himself.

27: Jimmy Rimmer is the only player to have won European Cup winners medals with two different English clubs. (Manchester United in 1968 and Aston Villa in 1982)

28: There has been at least one Bayern Munich player in the final of the World Cup since 1982.

29: Laszlo Kubala is the only player recognised by FIFA to have played for three different countries.(This is no longer allowed.) He played for Czechoslovakia, Hungary and Spain.

30: In Gaelic Pittodrie, the home of Scottish club Aberdeen translates roughly to Shit-heap.

31: Before Alex Ferguson became Manchester United manager, Aston Villa were a more successful club.

32: The word Soccer was actually derived in England.

33: Liverpool goalkeeper Simon Mignolet has a degree in politics and is fluent in 5 languages.

34: Dundee United have a 100% record against footballing giants Barcelona after playing them and winning 4 times in competitive matches.

35: St Johnstone has the distinction of being the only team in the top 4 divisions of either England or Scotland with a J in their name.

36: In his Iceland debut Eidur Gudjohnson came on as a sub replacing his father.

37: The first World Cup was won by Uruguay

G Is For.....Golf

1: There are 125,000 golf balls every year that get hit into the lake at the 17th hole of the Stadium Course at Sawgrass.

2: The word Caddy is derived from the French word Cadet which means "Youngest child."

3: Doug Ford entered a contest in which he correctly predicted his own victory in 1957 as well as his score of 282.

4: The average walking distance of an 18-hole course is 4 miles.

5: Until the invention of the golf tee balls ere hit of sand piles that the golfer made for themselves.

6: Golf is one of only two sports that have been played on the moon. The other is Javelin throwing.

7: A golf ball will travel further on a hot day.

8: Golf balls used to be made of leather and chicken feathers.

9: 80% of golfers will never achieve a handicap less than 18.

10: Tiger Woods has won 79 PGA tournaments including 14 Majors.

11: The term "birdie" comes from an American named Ab Smith. While playing a round of golf in 1899, he played what he described as a "bird of a shot", which became "birdie" over time.

12: A Birdie is one shot under Par.

13: Two shots under par is an Eagle

14: Three Shots under par is known as an Albatross.

15: One Two and Three shots over par are known as Bogie, Double-Bogie and Triple Bogie.

16: Golfer Arnold Palmer as nicknamed "The King".

17: Tiger Woods has won over $100m in prize money.

18: Rory McIlroy won the US Open in 2011 by 8 shots with an impressive score of -16.

19: The only tournament won by Ian Woosnam was the 1991 US Masters.

20: Jack Nicklaus won the masters an outstanding 6 times.

21: The longest recorded drive was a gigantic 515 yards this was achieved by Michael Hoke Austin in September 1974.

22: The first women's tournament was held on New Years Day 1811.

23: In 1976 Bob Cook sank a putt measured at 140 feet and 2,75 inches.

24: The women's equivalent of the Ryder Cup is named the Solheim Cup.

25: Tom Watson won the British Open 5 times.

26: Ernie Els is nicknamed "The Big Easy".

27: St Andrews golf course was established in 1552.

28: There are 336 dimples on a regulation golf ball.

29: the longest ever Putt is a huge 375 feet.

30: The largest bunker in the world is Hell's Half Acre on the 585-yard 7th hole of the Pine Valley Course in New Jersey.

31: Phil Mickelson plays left-handed which is impressive considering he is right-handed.

32: In March 1961, Lou Kretlow got the longest hole-in-one at the 427 yards 16th hole at Lake Hefner course, Oklahoma City, USA

33: In 1457 King James II of Scotland banned golf as it distracted soldiers from archery.

H Is For....Horse Racing

1: The average race horse weighs around 453kg.

2: The Grand National gets 10m viewers from around the world.

3: Horse racing is steadily growing in popularity each year.

4: No horse over the age of 18 has ever won a race.

5: When a horse retires from racing they can go on to be a dressage horse. One great example is former racing great Kauto Star.

6: The ancient Roman chariot racing is the earliest known form of an organised horse race.

7: The lowest weight a jockey has reached is 2st 11lb. This was in 1840 and the jockey was a man named Kitchener.

8: Humorist, The horse that on the Epsom Derby in 1921 only had one lung.

9: The oldest ever thoroughbred Tango Duke died in 1978 at the grand old age of 42.

10: In 1932 jockey Levi Barlingume ran his last competitive race he was 80 years old.

11: In 1908 a plough horse won the grand national.

12: Around £72bn ($100bn) is bet on horse racing each year.

13: Successful stallions can earn more money from being a stud horse than a racehorse.

14: A racehorses ancestry can be traced to Arab horses being bred with English horses.

15: Thoroughbred horses have doubled in size when compared to Arab racehorses from a thousand years ago.

16: Jockey Eddie Arcaro who won 4,779 races in his career lost his first 250 races.

17: One jockey had to lose 14lb in one day to achieve the required weight to ride his horse and succeeded. The jockey was a man named Alfred Johnson.

18: The slowest winning time as achieved in a 2-mile race in 1945 when Never Mind II finished in 11m 28s.

19: Every racehorse has its birthday on New Years Day regardless of when it was born.

20: The elastic V-shaped pad of soft horn in the middle of the sole of a horse's hoof, which helps absorb the impact when walking, is called a 'frog'.

21: The Legendary Red Rum is one of the most beloved horses to ever come out of the sport of racing and won the Grand National an impressive 3 times.

I Is For.....Ice Hockey

1: The history of the origins of Ice Hockey is continually disputed. One version has it invented in the 1700s by the French. While an opposing version says it was invented in the 1800s by the Canadians.

2: Before 1927 forward passes were not allowed in ice hockey.

3: The first organised indoor hockey game was played at Montreal's Victoria Skating Rink. It took place on 3rd March 1875.

4: In 1974 former Pittsburgh Penguins goal tender Andy Brown was the last person to not wear a mask in that position.

5: Former Chicago Blackhawks player Stan Mikita is credited with the curved stick blade in the 1960s (It was previously straight).

6: The NHL as founded on 22nd November 1917.

7: The tradition of fans waving white towels during playoff games was started when then–Vancouver Canucks coach Roger Neilson waved a towel on the end of a stick at a referee during a game in 1982, as a cheeky sign that he was giving up after a number of questionable calls.

8: The fastest slap shot in NHL history (Using a regulation puck) was a staggering 108.8 MPH this as achieved by Zideno Chara

9: There are at least 12 women with their name engraved on the Stanley Cup.

10: In the 1974 NHL Draft, Buffalo Sabres GM Punch Imlach decided to fool the media and league officials by drafting Taro Tsujimoto of the Japanese Hockey League's Tokyo Katanas. Trouble was, neither Tsujimoto nor his team was real. The pick was later stricken from the records.

11: In 1949 the first self-propelled ice-clearing machine was invented by Frank Zamboni.

12: Ron Hextall was the first goal tender to score a goal.

13: The first goal in the NHL as scored on 19th December 1917 by Montreal Wanderers player Dave Ritchie against Toronto Arenas.

14: In 1971 the first $1m contract was signed when Bobby Orr signed a 5-year deal worth $200,000 a year with the Boston Bruins.

15: The Disney film "The Mighty Ducks" inspired the name of the Anaheim Ducks (Originally Anaheim Mighty Ducks.).

16: The original Stanley Cup was only 7 inches tall.

17: Since 1914 the Stanley Cup has been won yearly. There are only two years it has not been awarded 1919 Ad 2005.

18: A hockey puck has a diameter of 3 inches.

19: Darryl Sittler holds the NHL record for most points scored in a game with 10 points (6 goals and 4 assists.)

20: The standard North American ice rink is 200ft long and 85ft wide.

21: Wayne Gretzky holds the record for most NHL records held with 61.

22: The Stanley Cup has had many adventures since its creation in 1893. Through the years, it has been used as a cereal bowl, accidentally left by the side of the road, tossed into a swimming pool and even lost, like luggage, on a 2010 flight from New Jersey to Vancouver. It was later recovered by an Air Canada employee.

23: The layer of ice in a pro hockey rink is usually three-quarters of an inch thick and is kept at a temperature of -9 degrees Celsius.

24: 12 Hall of Famer's featured in the 1956 Montreal Canadians team.

25: A Goalkeeper cannot touch the puck on the opposite side of the centre line.

26: In 1992, goalie Manon Rhéaume became the first woman to play in the NHL, suiting up for the Tampa Bay Lightning during an exhibition game.

27: To prevent bouncing hokey pucks are frozen before games.

28: Joe Malone holds the record for most goals in a single game with 7. He achieved this on 31st January 1920 while playing for Quebec Bulldogs against Toronto St Pats.

29: The Stanley Cup is named after a former Canadian Governor General, Lord Stanley of Preston, who donated the trophy in 1893.

30: In 1932 the Maple Leaf Gardens arena became the first to have a 4-sided clock.

31: In Detroit, fans often throw an octopus on the ice during the playoffs, when the Red Wings score. The tradition dates back to the Original Six era when it only took eight wins (one for every octopus tentacle) to capture the Stanley Cup.

J Is For...Jokgu

1: Jokgu is a combination of football (soccer) and volleyball.

2: Jokgu is a Korean sport.

3: Jokgu was invented in 1960 by members of the Republic of Korea Air Force.

4: In Korea, there are over one thousand Jokgu teams.

5: Some regard Jokgu as Korea's national sport.

6: Jogku is one of the sports that were premiered at the 1st Annual Leisure Games in Chuncheon, Korea in 2010.

7: The word Jokgu derives from the Chinese words for foot (Jok) and ball (Gu)

8: Jokgu is played on a court similar to a tennis.

9: Jokgu can be played on almost any flat surface using a small net.

K Is For....Kubb

1: Kubb is known as sticky sticks in English.

2: Kubb is a game played on almost any surface.

3: The object of the game is to throw wooden batons at wooden blocks in an attempt to knock them over.

4: The playing area of Kubb is rectangular.

5: The blocks known as Kubbs are placed on either end of the rectangle and then the king (A bigger block) is placed in the middle.

6: Kubb is believed to have its origins linked with the Vikings(This is debatable).

7: Kubb is also sometimes referred to as Viking Chess.

8: Kubb is a mix of cricket, bowling and horseshoes.

9: The object of Kubb is to knock over the opposing Kubb's and then the king over before your opponent.

10: Commercial Kubb sets were not manufactured until the 1980s.

11: The first World Championships was held in 1995.

12: The US National Kubb championship has been held in Wisconsin since 2007.

13: The largest weekly Kubb league is the Eau Claire Club League.

L Is For.....Lacrosse

1: Lacrosse is said to be the fastest game on two feet.

2: Lacrosse was invented by Native Americans.

3: Along with the Native Americans the French helped set the foundations of the sport.

4: The game was originally used to toughen up men to prepare them for war.

5: Indian Lacrosse was often played with a huge number of people meaning there could be anything up to 1,000 players.

6: In the summer of 1763, lacrosse was played by 2 tribes to distract British soldiers, in order to recapture Fort Michilimackinac.

7: The first women's Lacrosse game took place in Scotland in 1890.

8: The rules were created in 1794 when a game between the Seneca and Mohawks tribes was played.

9: In its best days Lacrosse as considered the most widely played team-sport in the North American continent. Its popularity continues to steadily grow.

M Is For....Motocross/Supercross

1: Motocross is a form of off-road motorcycle racing held on enclosed off-road circuits.

2: Motocross was first evolved in the U.K. from motorcycle trials competitions, such as the Auto-Cycle Clubs's first quarterly trial in 1909 and the Scottish Six Days Trial that began in 1912.

3: The first ever official scramble was held in Surrey, England in 1924.

4: Freestyle Motocross FSM started in the 1990s

5: Jeremy McGrath holds the record for most Supercross wins. With 72.

6: Ricky Carmichael holds the record for most Supercross/motocross wins combined with a total of 150. No other rider has even reached 100.

7: Ricky Carmichael and James Stewart share the record for most Motocross wins in a single season with 24.

8: Ricky Carmichael holds the record for lapping the most riders in a race with 39.

9: In 1974 Marty Tripes set the record for the youngest ever winner of a supercross he was 16y and 10 days old.

10: Motocross was originally raced with a 500cc engine.

11: The 250cc engine was introduced in 1957.

12: In 1975 the 125cc dicipline was introduced.

13: The first Motocross World Championships (500cc) was held in 1952 and as won by Belgian born Victor Leloup.

14: Belgium had at least one representative in the top 3 in 4 out of the first 5 Motocross World Championships.

15: Belgium almost had the clean sweep at the first ever 500cc Motocross World Championships, however, Britains John Avery spoiled their party finishing third. Belgium did achieve the clean sweep in 1953, 1954., 1991, 2001 and 2006.

16: The only other country to have achieved a clean sweep in the 500cc Motocross World Championships is Sweden. They achieved it in 1960, 1961,1962 and 1970

17: The three most successful countries in the 500cc Motocross World Championships are Belgium (24) Sweden (10) and Great Britain (6)

18: Belgium have been the most successful producer of winning riders across all 3 Motocross World Championship disciplines 500cc (24) 250cc (18) and 125cc (10)

19: Great Britain achieved the clean sweep (1st 2nd and 3rd) in the 250cc Motocross World Championships. They achieved this in 1961

20: Belgium is the only other country with a clean sweep in the 250cc discipline hen they achieved it in 1970

21: The first ever winner of the 250cc Motocross World Championships was German Fritz Betzelbacher in 1957.

22: The 3 most successful countries in the 250cc discipline are Belgium (18) Italy (9) and France (8)

23: Italy is the only country to have achieved a clean sweep n the 125cc discipline of the Motocross World Championships. They achieved it in 1957.

24: in 1972 Belgian Gaston Rahier became the first ever winner of the 125cc discipline.

25: The three most successful countries in the 125cc discipline of the Motocross World Championships are Belgium (10) Italy (7) and France (7)

26: Across all 3 disciplines of the Motocross World Championships Belgium have won the most medals by far with an impressive haul of 135 (55 gold 46 silver and 34 bronze) This eclipses their nearest rivals Sweden who have 55.

N Is For....Netball

1: Netball was created in England in 1893.

2: The first time Netball as played in the commonwealth games was in 1998.

3: The Netball goalpost stands at 3.85m tall

4: New Zealand's national team are known as the Silver Ferns.

5: The Australian national team are known as the Diamonds.

6: In England Netball is not considered a professional sport and most players have other jobs too.

7: The ANZ Championship lasted 9 seasons (the 8 years between 2008-2016) Only 10 teams ever competed in it (5 from Australia and 5 from New Zealand.)

8: The first Netball World Championships were held in 1963 it took place in Eastbourne, England.

9: Martina Bergman-Osterberg introduced netball as a female version of basketball.

10: Madame Ostenburg's College in England held the first official Netball game in 1895.

11: There are only 5 positions allowed in the centre third.

12: If a high-stakes match ends in a tie then the match continues until one team has a two-point lead.

13: Each team consists of 7 players.

14: The first ever World Series Netball competition was held in 2009.

15: The first match of the ANZ Championship in 2008 was contested between Central Pulse and Melbourne Vixens. The Melbourne Vixens won with a score of 50-33.

16: A player can legally hold the ball for up to 3 seconds.

17: The Australian National Competition started life out as the Esso Super League and began in 1985.

18: Sharelle McMahon scored the winning goal for Australia in the 1999 World Championships.

19: Melbourne Phoenix won the Commonwealth Bank Trophy in 2002. They beat the Thunderbirds in the final.

20: A professional Netball game is played with a size 5 ball.

21: There are two positions that can shoot for goals they are Goal Shooter (GS) and Goal Attack (GA).

22: Manchester, England hosted the first World Series Netball competition.

23: After a team scores the ball is taken back to the centre.

24: The Netball World Championships is held every 4-years.

25: Netball umpires generally wear white.

O Is For....Orienteering

1: The governing body of the sport (IOF) is based in Finland.

2: The scale of a map used in orienteering is 1:15,000

3: The man credited with being the father of orienteering is a Swedish man who was a scout leader named Ernst Killander.

4: On orienteering maps magnetic North rather than true North is indicated.

5: The contour interval is 5 meters.

6: On an orienteering map a triangle represents the starting point.

7: The flags marking a control point on the course are usually white and orange.

8: Children are trained on a course known as the string course.

9: A control point where competitors both arrive and leave by the same way is called a dog-leg.

10: On an orienteering map the finish is marked with a double circle.

11: Flags are left on the ground to let competitors know they have reached the right spot.

12: To prove that they have reached a checkpoint the competitor has to punch a hole into a card.

P Is For...Polo

1: As well as the traditional Polo played using horses there are variants such as Elephant Polo.

2: In Nepal, Elephant Polo is played under the World Elephant Polo Association. (WEPA)

3: There are 4 players on a Polo team.

4: A normal game of Polo is split into 4 periods of time these are known as Chukkas.

5: A Chukka is usually around 7.5 minutes long.

6: Elephant Polo only consists of two Chukkas. These last 10 minutes with a 15-minute break in-between.

7: In Polo a players horses are called Polo Ponies.

8: India developed Alternative Elephant Polo (AEP) these matches take place on Winter evenings.

9: If you get a Penalty 1 against you that is an automatic goal for your opponents.

10: In Sri Lanka in 2007 One of the Spanish teams elephants went on a rampage and crushed the minibus after throwing off his rider. The elephant named Abey is said to have got "Confused".

11: The bridle that most players use is called a gag.

12: A game of Polo has 3 umpires.

13: In Polo a backup girth is called a Surcingle.

14: The 2008 American team practised for Elephant Polo using Cadillac SUVs in Jacob Riis Park located in Queens, New York, USA.

15: Polo originated in Ancient Egypt and was originally played on foot.

16: Persia is the birthplace of Polo as e know it today. In the 6th Century, the Persian horsemen adapted the game to be played on horseback.

17: The Persians named the game horse-ball.

18: There is a monument in the Bazaar of Lahore in Pakistan. IT is a memorial to the first ever fatal Polo accident. It occurred in 1210.

19: The first modern PoloClub was established in 1862. (The Calcutta Polo Club).

20: During the 1910s America had their own version of Polo called Auto Polo which was played using cars.

21: Polo was an Olympic sport for 39 years (1930-1939)

22: The size of a Polo field is 300yrds by 160yrds.

23: According to the UPA You cannot play Polo left-handed and only right-handed people can play.

Q Is For....Quoits

1: Quoits is a game similar to that of ring toss.

2: The stick you have to throw the rings at is called a hob.

3: For every ring that encircles the hob the thrower receives 2 points.

4: Like in Bowls(lawn) the thrower gets 1 point fo every ring that is closer to the hob than the opponents.

5: The rings are made of iron, rope or rubber.

6: The origins of the sport is said to be in Medieval England when for fun people would heat and bend horseshoes into a ring shape and toss it at an iron pegs that were driven into the ground.

R Is For….Rugby (All Disciplines)

1: In 2001 Welsh fly-half Neil Jenkins became the first player to reach 1,000 international points.

2: In 2005 during a test match against Uruguay, South African wing Tonderai Chavanga scored 6 tries.

3: Although Argentina have a jaguar on their crest a mistake by a South African journalist lead to them gaining the nickname "The Pumas"

4: In the 2007 Super 14 final Bryan Habana scored the winning try with time up on the clock.

5: The 2007 Hong Kong Sevens tournament was won by Samoa.

6: A scissor move can also be called a switch.

7: Rugby Union has a set piece called a Line out this does not appear in Rugby League.

8: The top try scorer at the 2003 Super 12 tournament was Doug Howlett with 12 tries in 13 games.

9: The Scrum-half is the link player between the forward line and the back line.

10: A rare Rugby Union book by J R Henderson called "The New Zealand Tour 1901" Depicts the journey of the New South Wales team.

11: There are two props in the team they are called loose-head and tight-head.

12: Props wear the numbers 1 and 3.

13: England was the last nation to play South Africa before their ban in 1977 due to the Gleneagles Agreement.

14: Joel Stransky scored the winning drop goal in the 1995 World Cup.

15: In 1993 James Small became the first Springbok to receive a red card.

16: A player playing wing position does not get involved in the scrum.

17: Numbers are usually relevant to positions. Such as the Lock who wears the number 4.

18: When a ball crosses the sideline it is said to be in touch.

19: Author J B G Thomas has written 30 books based on Rugby.

20: In Rugby Union, the player who throws the ball in from a line out is the hooker.

21: Twickenham is often considered as the home of Rugby and is known as the cabbage patch.

22: When the ball is dropped forward it is called a knock on.

23: Will Carling was known as Bumface.

24: In March 1871 Scotland beat England to win the first ever rugby international match.

25: England won the 2003 World Cup with an overtime drop goal.

26: South African winger Bryan Habana had 2 100m races with a cheetah in 2007. He was given a 30m head-start and lost both races.

27: Wales play their international home games at the Millenium Stadium.

28: There are officials called touch judges whose job it is to determine where the ball is carried out of bounds.

29: The purpose of a scrum is to put the ball back into play.

30: The hooker wears the number 2

31: England's Jonny Wilkinson scored the most points during the 2003 Rugby World Cup. He scored 113 points in 6 matches.

32: A conversion is worth 2 points.

33: Flankers wear the numbers 6 and 7.

34: A flanker used to be known as a wing-forward.

35: There are two flankers called the Openside and the blindside.

36: Carisbrook is known as the house of pain.

37: The first try of the 1991 World Cup was scored by Michael Jones.

38: Former New Zealand Rugby captain Sean Fitzpatrick had half his ear bitten off by South African rugby player Johan Le Roux in 1994.

39: The first national rugby team to win 18 consecutive test matches was Lithuania.

40: In 2010 Thom Evans suffered a severe neck injury forcing his retirement from the game.

41: There are 5 ways to score in Rugby they are A Try, Conversion, Drop goal, Penalty goal and a penalty try.

42: Commentator Bill McLaren was known as the voice of rugby.

43: In the first test match between Manu Samoa and Fiji there was a tree in the centre of the park.

44: Scotland has never beaten the All Blacks.

45: The first Australian international jersey colour was green.

46: A Scrum-half is often the shortest player on the pitch, and they wear the number 9.

47: John Eales' nickname is Nobody. This is because as they say "Nobody is perfect".

48: Ellis Park hosted the 1995 Rugby World Cup final between The All Blacks and the Springboks.

49: In a 1981 test match between South Africa and New Zealand All Black player Gary Knight was hit with a flour bomb.

S Is For....Snooker

1: Snooker is said to have been devised in 1875 by bored army officers in India experimented with variations on billiards.

2: Sir Neville Chamberlain is said to be the creator of the sport.

3: While playing in the 1980 World Team Cup challenge, heavy-set Canadian player Bill Werbeniuk split his trousers while playing live on TV. The incident was made worse by him not wearing underpants.

4: Under the official rules of snooker, the referee shall, if a player is colour blind, tell him the colour of a ball if requested.

5: The game originally included 15 reds, yellow, green, pink and black.

6: Joe Davis won just £6.10s.0d after becoming the first world champion in 1927.

7: The word 'snooker', a slang military term referring to someone who is inexperienced, became tied to the game after Chamberlain called an opponent a 'snooker' after he missed a pot.

8: Tony Drago holds the record for the quickest century break in tournament play. He took just 3 minutes31 seconds to make the 100 points.

9: The record for the fastest 147 maximum break in the game's history is held by rocket Ronnie O'Sullivan who made his clearance in five minutes and 20 seconds at the World Championship in 1997.

10: The white ball is known as the cue ball.

11: A common term for when the cue ball is potted is scratching. Thhis comes from when scores were kept on a blackboard.

12: The cue chalk actually contains no chalk.

13: The first female snooker champion was a man who had a 25yr career in the game his true identity was revealed after his death

14: There are 22 balls on the snooker table at the start of a frame.

15: The 1983 Professional Players Tournament was won by Tony Knowles.

16: Ronnie O'Sullivan won his first World Championship in the 200-2001 season beating John Higgins in the final.

17: John Parrott won the 1991 Embassy World Championship in 1991 beating Jimmy White in the final.

18: Stephen Hendry won the World Championship 7 times including winning 5 in a row.between 1992-1996.

19: Mark Williams won the 2003 LG Cup.

20: Stephen Hendry won his first World Championship in 1990.

21: Dennis Taylor beat Steve Davis to win the 1985 Embassy World Snooker Championship.

22: Ronnie O'Sullivan made his first maximum break in a tournament at the age of 15.

23: Jimmy White won the 1992 UK Championship.

24: Alex Higgins made history in the 1972 World Championships winning it in his first appearance at the tournament.

25: In 2007 Judd Trump became the youngest player to make a maximum break In tournament play at the World Championships. He was 14 years old.

T Is For....Tennis

1: In 1932 Henry Austin became the first person to wear shorts at Wimbledon.

2: Arthur Ashe was the first black man to win the US Open.

3: Tennis was removed from the Olympics in 1924 after being included since 1896. It was reinstated in 1988.

4: The first patented version of tennis, lawn tennis, was given the name Sphairistike. It was created by Major Walter Clopton and patented in 1874.

5: Rectangular courts were created in 1875 for Wimbledon. Originally, the court was an hour-glass shape.

6: In 1997 the maximum length of a racquet was changed from 32inches to 29inches.

7: For the first one hundred years that modern tennis was played, the strings of the racquets were made from the guts of animals.

8: The US Open trophy is made by Tiffany & Co.

9: The first winner at Wimbledon was Spencer Gore. He didn't think the game would catch on.

10: In 1498, Charles VIII of France hit his head on the door of a primitive tennis court and died.

11: Sabine Lisicki has the fastest recorded serve for women at 210km/h.

12: Venus Williams and her sister Serena both won Olympic gold medals for tennis. They are the first set of sisters to accomplish this.

13: Women who played in the first Wimbledon tournaments had to wear full-length dresses.

14: Tennis originated in 12th Century France and was originally played hitting the ball with the palm of your hand.

15: If a player ins all 4 majors in their career they are said to have achieved a career Grand Slam.

16: The Davis Cup started in 1900.

17: The tie-break was invented by James Van Alen in 1965.

18: Don Budge is the only male player to have won 6 consecutive Grand Slam singles titles.

19: Australian Sam Groth had the fastest serve for men recorded at a speed of 263.44km/h

20: The term love meaning 0 is said to have originated from the French term for egg because on the scoreboard the 0 looks like an egg.

21: A Harris Hawk named Rufus is stationed near Wimbledon to keep the skis clear of pigeons.

22: Ivo Karlovic holds the record for most Aces with 12,196.

23: Roger Federer holds the record for career prize money earned with £79,745,399.18 ($107,560,560) and counting.

24: The ATP as formed in 1972.

25: Tennis balls were originally white.

U Is For....Ulama

1: Ulama is the oldest known team sport in the world.

2: During the pre-Columbian era the game used to be tied to human sacrifice.

3: Tha Mayan people used to call the sport Pok a Tok.

4: The Aztec people used to callit Tlachtli.

5: The game used to be played on stone courts.

6: The game was so brutal it would often end in serious injury and death.

7: The earliest known court is Paso de la Amada in Mexico.

8: The Olmec courts were generally the size of modern day football fields.

9: The field was shaped like a capital I

10: The courts were lined with stone blocks and played on a rectangular court with slanted walls. These walls were often plastered and brightly painted. Serpents, jaguars, raptors were depicted alongside images of human sacrifice suggesting a connection to the divinity.

11: Nobody knows for sure the full rules of the game played by the Meso-Americans.

12: The ball used was about the size of a basketball and could weigh up to 8 pounds.

13: It is similar in objective to that of volleyball.

V Is For.....Volleyball

1: William G Morgan invented Volleyball in 1895.

2: The first men's World Championship was held in 1949

3: The first women's World Championships was held in 1952.

4: The longest volleyball game lasted 75h 30m

5: Volleyball is the second most popular sport in the world.

6: The first ball specially designed for volleyball was made in 1900.

7: Volleyball was introduced to the Olympic games in Tokyo 1964.

8: On average a volleyball player jumps 300 times every match.

9: Volleyball was originally called Mintonette.

10: The first 2-man beach volleyball game took place in 1930.

11: Volleyball was invented in America.

12: The first Volleyball game was played at Springfield College on 7th July 1896.

13: A volleyball court is 29ft 6in wide and 59ft long.

14: The USVBA (Now USA Volleyball.) was formed in 1928.

15: In 1916, the skills of set and spike were originated during a match in the Philippines.

16: The FIVB was created in 1947.

17: Until 1920 Volleyball was an indoor only sport.

18: During the summer of 1976, at Will Rogers State Beach, the first professional beach volleyball tournament took place. It was called the "Olympia World Championship of Beach Volleyball".

19: Yasutaka Matsudaira described volleyball as being "Like an orchestra sent from heaven."

20: Al Scates is the first college volleyball coach to reach 900 wins.

21: The Floater serve is very similar to a knuckle ball in baseball. Its unpredictable movement can cause the opposing team to fall over trying to hit it.

W Is For.....Weight lifting

1: Bulgaria is a weight lifting super power.

2: There are two types of lift. The snatch and the clean & Jerk.

3: North Korea won 3 gold medals at the London Olympics in 2012.

4: Weightlifting was first introduced to the Olympic Games in 1896.

5: Competitors have 3 chances to lift a weight.

6: In competitions there are 3 judges that cast their eyes over each lift.

7: The 2000 Olympics was the first time that women were allowed to compete at the Olympics in weightlifting.

8: Ibragim Samadov, who represented the Unified Team at the 1992 Olympics weightlifting, finished in equal first in the 82.5 kg division, but was relegated to 3rd on a countback due to him being 0.05 kg heavier. In protest, he refused to lean forward to accept his medal, instead took it in his hand then dropped it. The IOC subsequently disqualified him.

9: The best all-time performing Weightlifting athlete at the Olympic Games is Pyrros Dimas of Greece with three gold medals and one bronze.

10: In the early Olympics there was no weight classes in the weight lifting.

11: Until 1964 it was illegal for the bar to touch the legs or hips during a lift.

12: The first women's World Championship took place in 1987.

X Is For....Xare

1: Xare is a sport that involves a racquet and ball.

2: Xare is a form of Basque Pelota.

3: Xare is very popular in South American countries.

4: The court for Xare consists of 4 walls.

5: The left wall of the court features a facade, about 2ft wide with a slanting roof.

6: The strings on a Xare racquet are like woven mesh.

7: The game is played with two competing teams of 2 players per team.

8: Matches are played in a points and sets format.

Y Is For....Yukigassen

1: Yukigassen was invented in Japan.

2: Yukigassen is played between 2 teams of 7 players.

3: There are annual tournaments in Japan, Finland, Norway, Australia, Sweden, United States, and Canada.

4: All snowballs are made to specific standards in the machines provided so the game is fair and safe.

5: Yukigassen is a mixture of dodge ball paintball and capture the flag.

6: Players wear special yukigassen helmets with face shields,

7: There are 90 Snowballs made in advance of a game.

Z Is For...Zui Quan

1: Zui Quan is also known as Drunken fist or Drunken boxing.

2: Zui Quan gets its name from the fact its style of movement imitates a drunk person.

3: Zui Quan is considered the most difficult style of Wushu you can learn.

4: It requires great balance and coordination.

5: Strong joints and fingers are crucial for Zui Quan.

6: Zui Quans origins are traced back to Buddhist and Daoist sects (618-907 AD).

7: The main body method is called Sloshing.

8: Swaying and falling with momentum are major methods used to fight in Zui Quan.

9: The main hand gesture in Zui Quan is to imitate holding a small cup of Wine.

Printed in Great Britain
by Amazon